Boundaries

Boundaries

Staying Pure in Your Teenage Years

Becky Legatt

HighWay
A division of Anomalos Publishing House
Crane

HighWay

A division of Anomalos Publishing House, Crane
65633
Printed in the United States of America

09   1

ISBN-10: 0982036183 (cloth)
EAN-13: 9780982036181 (cloth)

A CIP catalog record for this book is available from
the Library of Congress.

Cover illustration and design by Steve Warner

All scripture quotes are from the New International
Version.

Contents

1
My Story

I grew up in a small town, where we had two official churches: a Catholic church and a Lutheran church. My family belonged to the Catholic Church. If you would have asked me growing up if I was a Christian, I would have replied, "I am Catholic." The term Christian was foreign to me. The term I was familiar with was "religion." Everyone had a religion they belonged to—a religion from which they did not dare switch. It was almost like a social status. We thought our way was right and the way of other religions was wrong. Strangely, I never knew what the differences were; I just knew we were right.

Even though my family carried the Catholic label with honor, we still only went to church on Christmas and Easter. As long as you made it to Mass on those two days, you were good. However, we could never miss religion class because my parents wanted to make sure that we would one day get confirmed in the Catholic Church. It was all about knowing the right things to say and do. It was not about a relationship with God; it was about rituals. I am not saying that all Catholic churches are this way. I have heard of many Catholic churches where the people have a strong relationship with God, but that was not the way I felt when I was growing up. My family never read the Bible. The only time I remember reading the Bible was when we were young and my dad would read the creation story to us from one of those big, white Holy Bibles. During Mass they would read two scriptures, but neither ever made sense to me. The only prayers we prayed were those we had memorized. Even at home we only prayed the memorized prayers for blessing the food, and I always messed up which hand to use to sign Father, Son, and Holy Spirit.

Since we read very little of the Bible, I did not know much about Jesus. What I did know was that Jesus was everywhere and that I could talk to Him anytime, but I did not know why He would want to talk to me. All I knew about Him was rules, not relationship. The one thing I really dreaded was the one Saturday each month when we had to go to confession. Basically, I had to think of all the rules I had broken that month and confess them to the Priest in an old-smelling, confined room. I felt like I was walking into a dungeon.

My whole religious experience revolved around knowing the rules, so I could ask for forgiveness from them when I broke them. On top of that, the Priest would give me penance for breaking the rules. For instance, he might tell me to wash the dishes that week for my mom and say ten Hail Mary's, or something similar. I never understood why I had to tell the Priest I sinned so I could go home and do chores.

As I grew older, I fought with my parents about religion classes and confession. I never won the religion class battle, but eventually I did not have to go to confession. In religion class, we learned about the Ten Commandments and the descendants from Adam. I learned a lot of interesting things, but I never understood why we did what we did or believed what we believed. This confusion led right into my dating life. Our church taught us not to have sex before marriage. However, it never taught us why we should not have sex before marriage. Again, to me this was just another rule. Rules were meant to be broken so we had something to confess. Sex was also one of those taboo things that families didn't talk about. I love my parents dearly, but they never had meaningful conversations about sex or relationships until it was too late.

At that point in my life I was confused about God and did not know what God wanted from me. I just tried to please my family and be a good little girl and do what I was told. I thought that to go to heaven when you died required occasionally attending church and generally being a good person. However, deep down inside I felt empty. I had a longing for something, but I did not know what.

As I got older I tried to fill my emptiness with approval from teachers, men, and my peers. I always tried to do my best in everything. I wanted to be the teacher's pet and I thought that would make me cool. Instead, it only caused the cool people to partner with me in class so they would do well on projects. They never picked me because they liked me. Therefore, I tried to win approval with guys.

I started becoming interested in boys in fifth grade, and had my first boyfriend around that time. We only saw each other in school, but it is amazing what can be done at school. The biggest event of the day was on the shuttle bus from middle school to high school where we got on the bus to go home. It was about a four-minute drive, and we would sit in the back of the bus and have competitions to see which couple could kiss the longest. I really did not think it was a big deal at the time; hey, most of the time I won. I hoped maybe this would fill the emptiness, but it didn't. Do not get me wrong, I was not a bad child. I got good grades, I was respectful, and I obeyed most of the rules. I was mainly known as the smart, quiet girl, so kissing on the bus boosted my popularity and my visibility. I can now look back and see how dumb my actions were and how they did hurt me, but at the time I thought nothing of it—it was the cool thing to do on the bus.

After that first two-month relationship ended, I had boyfriends here and there, but nothing serious for two years. That changed in the seventh grade. I had liked a boy for some time, but he was taken (actually, he was dating one of my best friends). She had told me a lot about their relationship, including the fact that they'd had sex. They were only eleven years old, which to me should have been a big warning flag, but I thought, "Wow, this guy must be amazing if he was worth losing your virginity over." Later that year her mom died in a freak accident, and she and her boyfriend drifted apart until eventually they broke up on good terms. After awhile he asked me out, and I was so excited, but I made sure it was ok with my friend. I thought he was "all that and a bag of chips," as they say. I was the luckiest girl in the world. There was no way I could lose him. For a moment it felt like I had found what I was looking for; that no longer would I have to feel empty.

When we started dating, we did not discuss sex or sexual boundaries. We both knew that I knew about his past relationship, but we never talked about it. Until then I had always pictured myself being a virgin until I got married. Not because I had a conviction about God's will for my life, but because I was told it was the right thing to do. However, because I knew my boyfriend had already had sex, I felt like if I did not have sex with him he would not like me anymore. If he did not like me anymore, I thought the emptiness would return. So, at the age of twelve, I lost my virginity. Honestly, I did not like it. Sex hurt, and I felt like I had to continue having it to keep him happy. In addition, after the newness of the relationship wore off, the emptiness in my heart returned. I became an expert at faking it. It felt like something was missing (I know now it was God). I also had guilt that I could not seem to get away from, not to mention that I constantly worried about pregnancy because we rarely used condoms and I was too ashamed to talk to my parents in order to access birth control. I knew my parents loved me, and I loved them too. I loved them so much I did not want to disappoint them by telling them what I was doing.

I also did not want anyone else to discover that we were having sex, but things spread easily in a small town. Eventually, most of my peers caught on and my parents found out. Thankfully, I have great parents that chose to love me rather than judge me. The relationship between my boyfriend and me lasted nearly three years, until circumstances drew us apart. After we broke up, life removed the rose-colored glasses from my eyes and I was able to see the kind of person he really was. I felt dumb that for the past few years I had done everything to try and keep our relationship together. I gave him everything and got nothing but pain in return.

I needed time to heal from that relationship and was not interested in another. I had written boys off—I thought I would not date again until I was done with college. However, after a while I decided all boys were not that bad and again thought about dating. About four months after the break-up, a really nice, cute guy started working for my dad. Did I mention he had a nice truck? I told my sister I thought he was cute and she talked to him and it turned out he thought I was cute, too. Therefore in late June, Jonathan and I went on our first date. Jonathan brought me roses, opened doors for me, took me to a flower garden, and bought me dinner. At the flower garden we sat on a swing that looked out over the river and talked. I knew something was different about this guy. Soon after we started dating I found out what was different, what he had that I'd longed for all my life: a real relationship with God. In July of that year, I asked Jesus into my heart and started my own personal relationship with God. From that day on Jesus completely changed my life. Finally, I had found something that truly filled the emptiness inside.

However, I still had this issue of sexual

sin in my life. Even though I had just accepted Jesus into my life, I was still a baby Christian. I still knew that sex was wrong outside of marriage, but I did not know why. While I thought that since I was dating a Christian boy, sex would not be an issue, I soon found out that Christian boys have the same hormones as non-Christian boys. Things moved much faster than I thought they would: one thing led to another and soon we were making out. Therefore, when the relationship started getting serious, I thought he would expect me to have sex with him because he knew I was not a virgin. Eventually, we had sex. We never talked about how far we wanted to go; we just let our feelings lead us.

After we had sex, the same feelings of guilt and shame returned. Worse, I now felt like the bad guy. I knew how it felt for me to lose my virginity before I was married and now I had just taken Jonathan's. I was still very much in love with Jonathan, but I was worried he would resent me. Then, a month later it was my birthday and he gave me a promise ring. I was excited, but I did not understand fully what it meant. Deep down I felt he only wanted to marry me because I had taken his virginity. I did not think anyone would want me for who I was—having sex before I was married depleted my self worth; I felt dirty. I had accepted Jesus into my heart, but I still held onto my chains of bondage.

One biblical truth I learned in my adolescence was that anything done in the dark will be brought into the light. Not long after Jonathan gave me the promise ring, his parents found out we'd had sex. His parents were deeply hurt and told Jonathan he had to break up with me or move out. I thought for sure he would break up with me. However, he chose to move out and live with his sister, and later with my grandparents.

Jonathan and I continued dating through high school, and he continued living with my grandparents. Jonathan and I continued to attend church faithfully and grew in the Lord, but our sexual sin held us back from many of God's blessings. We knew what we were doing was wrong, but we didn't know how to stop. Every time we tried abstinence, we fell back into temptation.

Jonathan and I got engaged the Christmas of his senior year and my junior year. After Jonathan graduated he joined the Air Force. At first I was upset that he joined, because I did not want to move away from family and friends. However, this was a turning point in our relationship. Jonathan was gone to basic training and I was at home. I had time to reflect on our relationship and the things we were doing wrong. While Jonathan was in basic training, we both vowed to not have sex again until we were married. I felt huge freedom! I felt a burden lifted off of my shoulders. I finally felt clean and completely loved.

God worked with me a great deal through that summer. He showed me that my sin did not hurt only myself, but that it affected everyone around me, especially Jonathan's parents. Although our relationship was improving, it was still rocky. God showed me I had to tell them I was sorry for my sin that hurt them. I thought it was going to be one of the hardest things to do, but it was one of the most freeing things I have ever done. Jonathan's parents are so great; they forgave wholeheartedly and welcomed me as a daughter into their family.

After that summer, Jonathan returned home for relocating to his permanent duty station in Abilene, Texas. We were all geared up to stay sexually pure during this visit, but we did nothing to help make this happen. We talked about how we wanted to abstain from sex, but we had no plan to prevent sex. We did the same thing we always did and expected different results. It did not work. I once again failed myself. However, this time I had to put on an even bigger lie because everyone knew of our vow to abstain.

I wanted to get married so I could be free of my shame. I thought if we got married the past would not matter anymore. Therefore, we got married on December 27, 2001, by a Justice of the Peace in Abilene, Texas. Since I still wanted a ceremony in our church at home, with all the things I'd dreamed of as a girl, we stilled planed our wedding at home for June 21, 2002. Today that is the wedding anniversary we celebrate.

After getting married, we moved to

Abilene, TX, where Jonathan was stationed.
I began paging through the telephone book,
wishing to become involved immediately in
a local church. Of course, churches are in no
short supply in Abilene because it is a part
of the Bible Belt. However, there was one
name that stuck out: New Hope Church. After
the first Sunday, we knew we were home.
God did and is doing some amazing things
in our lives through that church. We learned
that getting married did not solve the issue
of sexual sin. We had to break the bondage
of sin over our sexual past. Many people
think that if they simply stop doing the wrong
things, everything will be alright. In truth, we
still need to repent for the sin from which
we have turned. I will discuss breaking the
bondage of sin in our lives more in chapter 4.

At New Hope Church I realized I did not
have to feel pain and guilt for my sin because
God had made me clean. Yes, I had fallen,

but he picked me up from the miry clay
and set me on a rock. Just like when I had
attempted to stay sexually pure the first time,
I felt free. I thought I could never feel that way
again because I had fallen after I promised
to stay pure. I learned that what I did was
wrong, but it was the action that God did not
like—He still loved **me**! My husband and I
repented of our sin, and that night, though
we had been together many times, it felt like
the first time because this time it was the way
God wanted it to be.

Jonathan and I were sad that we had
made bad choices when we were younger,
but we knew that Romans 8:28 says that,
"He promises to work all things for our good
for those who are in Christ Jesus." Jonathan
and I knew somehow God was going to
work this for good. One day Jonathan heard a
broadcast on Dr. Dobson about expectations
in relationships and how they need to be

discussed in all dating relationships. Later he came to me and we talked about our decisions when we were dating. It turned out that Jonathan did not want to have sex before marriage, but since he knew about my past he thought I expected him to have sex. And I did not want to have sex, but I thought since he knew about my past he would expect me to have sex. If we would have only talked about how we felt about sex we could have saved ourselves from a lot of bondage. We both realized how immature we were and how foolish our mistakes were. We did not talk about what our boundaries were until after we were married. From that moment on, we were determined to take what the devil meant for our destruction and turn it into good, by helping others to not make the same mistake we made.

Discussion Questions

1. What have you dealt with in the area of purity?

2. Can you think of the first time you learned about purity? Who talked to you about it? What did they say?

3. Did my story shock you? Are similar or worse things happening at your school?

2
How God Designed Sex

In order to help others not make the same mistake we made, we dove into God's word to find out what God says about sex. I knew that because God had a plan for sex, trusting what the world had to say about it was not the best idea. Sometimes we do things a certain way simply because that is the way we have always seen them done. Other times we do things in order to keep up with the times; trends, including sexual trends, are always changing. However, the awesome thing about God is that He never changes. Since the best way to find the true meaning of something is to go back to its beginning, we will start our journey in Genesis.

For this reason a man will leave his father and mother and be united to his wife, and they will become one flesh. The man and his wife were both naked, and they felt no shame.

GEN. 2:24-25

In this section of Genesis, God had just created our Earth and made man that he should rule over the land and animals. However, God found that none of the animals were suitable companions for man. Therefore, God made Adam to fall into a deep sleep and created woman from his rib.

He then commanded man to leave his father and mother be united to his wife, at which point they would become one flesh.

The key to understanding this passage is the first three words of verse 24: "For this reason." When I read this, I wondered what reason the Lord meant. When we look back, we see that in order for God to create a suitable companion for man, He had to take a rib from man. Man was now missing a part of himself. God knew man would never be complete without a woman because part of him was in her. Therefore, when the Bible says, "For this reason," it is referring to man missing a part of him. That is why God says after man and woman unite they become one flesh. This union puts the missing parts together to make one complete person. Apart, a man and a woman are not complete. It is like a puzzle: if just one piece is missing, the puzzle is incomplete. Not until you find the missing piece to the puzzle will the puzzle be complete.

Physically, the only act that can unite man and woman as one is sex. With today's culture we miss the importance of sex. Our culture sees sex as a means of personal pleasure. However, as we have seen in this passage, sex has a much deeper meaning. When you have sex with a person, you unite and become one. God said man should leave his father and mother and then unite; a command which speaks to marriage first, then sex. God intended men and women to be with only one partner because after they have sex, they have made a union of one flesh.

When you have physical relations with a person, you give up a part of yourself because you just became one flesh and are now trying to separate that union. However, as when you glue two pieces of paper together and try to tear them apart, you can never separate the sheets perfectly. Paul says, "Do you not know that he who unites himself with a prostitute is one with her in body? For it is said, 'The two will become one flesh'" (1 Cor. 6:16). When you have sex, part of you is left with that person, and again when you have sex with another person. Soon, you become a vague image of your original self because part of you is left with each of your sexual partners.

Not only do you leave part of yourself with each sexual partner you have had, you also collect part of them inside you. You are now part of them and they are part of you. One can see how that can really confuse an individual's identity after having several sexual partners. Can you imagine walking down the aisle on your wedding day with all of your sexual partners accompanying you at the altar because they are now a part of you? Then, they follow you right into your honeymoon suite for the duration of the evening. I know this illustration sounds funny, but I want you to be able to visualize what is happening at the spiritual level every time you have sex.

Another good illustration is Play-Doh. In our house, we have a rule that you can only play with one color at a time. If a child plays with two colors, the colors become mixed together and it is impossible to return them to their original state. Imagine that you are the color pink and your boyfriend or girlfriend is the color green. When you have sex it is like taking those two colors and mixing them. When you break up, you find it impossible to get back to your pink self. Sure, you can separate out some of the green, but you cannot get rid of it all. Thankfully, God provided a way to make you whole again. We'll discuss this concept later.

Let us take one last look at our passage from Genesis. We see that God commanded man and woman to marry and unite—and then the Lord talks about shame, "[They] were naked, and they felt no shame." When I was a new Christian and I read this passage, I always wondered why God had the author discuss shame. Why would a couple who had just had sex feel shame at seeing each other nude? After praying about this passage, the Lord showed me that when I had sex before I was married, I remember always feeling shame. I may have just had sex with him, but I now felt unclean and wanted to cover up. I never remembered a time before I was married that I did not feel shameful about the decisions I made. Then, God showed me that Adam and Eve did not feel shame because they had not sinned.

In Genesis, we do not see Adam and Eve experience shame until after they have

27

sinned. At that point their eyes become open and they realize they are naked. They quickly realize how unworthy they are to be in God's presence. When you have sex as a married couple, you feel no shame because there is no sin making you unworthy. When you have sex before marriage and allow sin in your life, you feel shame instead of joy as God intended.

Discussion Questions

1. Before reading this chapter, why did you think you should wait until you are married to have sex?

2. In this chapter, we read Genesis 2:24–25. Read it out loud again and discuss the new ways you view these verses in light of this chapter.

3. Take two pieces of Play-Doh of different colors and mix them together. What does this symbolize? Now try to separate them back to their original colors. Can it be done?

3
Why is Sex Different from Other Sins?

After I had accepted Christ as my personal savior, I knew and truly believed that God had forgiven all my sins. I also knew there was a lot of spiritual growing that had to happen in me. As badly as I wanted to be a mature believer the second I became saved, I wasn't, and it took work to get there. Part of my maturing processes happened when I would fall and the Lord would show me how to get up and get out of sin. As I mentioned earlier, sexual sin was so hard for me to escape. I kept falling, getting up, and falling again. I can now look back and see how good God was to me during those times. Even in my stubbornness, He was always there.

As I grew and matured, one question bothered me: Why, when I committed a sexual sin, did I feel so much worse than I did when I committed other sins? I did not understand, and I kept telling myself that all sin is sin, and that there is no level of severity in sin. So why did it feel worse? After I had gotten married and was studying sexuality in the Bible, God showed me why I felt this way:

Flee from sexual immorality. All other sins a man commits are outside his body, but he who sins sexually sins against his own body.

Do you not know that your body is a temple of the Holy Spirit, who is in you, whom you have received from God? You are not your own; you were bought at a price. Therefore, honor God with your body.

1 COR. 6:18–20

Verse 18 hits the nail on the head for me: "All other sins a man commits are outside his body, but he who sins sexually sins against his own body." The reason I felt worse after committing sexual sin was because I had sinned against both God and myself—it was a double whammy! When you mess with your body, you mess not only with the physical aspect but with the emotional and the spiritual aspect as well. The emotional and spiritual elements haunted me a great deal through my teenage years. I felt ashamed of my own actions and was not spiritually balanced.

I knew for a long time that there was a distance between God and me that I did not understand. The more I thought and prayed about this verse, God showed me spiritually what was happening when we commit sexual sins. Verse 19 says, "Do you not know that your body is a temple of the Holy Spirit, who is in you, whom you have received from God? You are not your own." Once we accept Christ as our savior, Christ comes and dwells within us. We are, as this verse states, temples of God. Our bodies are not our own; they are now God's bodies in which to dwell. The church is not a building, but the church is you and me and anyone who accepts Christ as their savior.

When you look at your body in this perspective, everything you do to your body you are in essence doing to God. Take a second to soak that in. Think about it in terms of sex. Whenever you sin against the body, you sin against God. Sex not only defiles your body, but it also defiles the God that dwells in you. Therefore, God flees from you because God and sin cannot co-exist. This explained the distance I felt; I could never have an intimate relationship with God because of my defilement. This short passage completely changed my thinking about sexual sin, and for the first time I stopped to think about it from God's perspective instead of my own.

The great thing about God is that when we do not understand something, when we ask God for understanding, He gives it to us. The other day I heard a teaching on the idols of the Old Testament, and God spoke to me. The two main idols of the Old Testament were Baal and Asher. I found out through this teaching that these idols were fertility gods, and people worshipped them by having sex in front of the idols. Pretty graphic I know, but it gets worse. After Solomon died, the kingdom of Israel spilt apart and things grew much worse. Soon, people were not worshipping God, but Baal and Asher. They brought their idols into the temple of God that Solomon had built and practiced their form of worship. I learned that prostitutes stayed at the temple so that people could come and "worship" at any time. Finally and unbelievably, any children produced from this worshiping were thrown into the fire as sacrifices to Baal and Asher.

God provided me with a powerful vision to illustrate this story. It is difficult for me to fathom people carrying out such misdeeds, especially in God's house. At that point, the Lord nudged me gently and told me that is exactly what we are doing when we engage in sexual immorality. Ouch! We are committing sin in God's house and reacting to it with a careless attitude. What happens to the babies that are produced from this union? Some are born and raised and live outstanding lives, but many others are aborted, their lives destroyed.

Discussion Questions

1. What are our bodies, according to 1 Corinthians 6:18–20?

2. Knowing what your bodies are after you accept Christ, how should this affect what we do with our bodies?

3. This chapter used some graphic images to portray what pre-marital sex looks like in the eyes of God. What correlations can you find between the worship of the false gods Baal and Asher and pre-marital sex?

4
Freedom

One mistake many teenagers make is thinking their actions don't affect anyone. How many times have you said or heard, "What is the big deal? I was not hurting anyone." The truth is we are hurting someone: we hurt ourselves by distancing ourselves from God. However, I have good news for everyone who has sinned (in other words, all of us). Jesus paid the price for our sins so we no longer need to live distanced from God.

Jesus took our dirty sins upon Himself, so we could have a relationship with God. The only thing we need to do to receive this gift is ask for it. If you have never asked Jesus to come into your life and take away your sins so that you can have a relationship with God, now is the time. Be honest, admit your sins, and accept forgiveness. The key then is to turn away from your sins. You should no longer willingly sin in God's temple. You have a choice to make when you wake up every morning—are you going to live for God or for yourself.

The enemy had told me one particular lie for years. The lie was that since I had already lost my virginity and could not get it back, it was no big deal if I did it again. Satan is the father of all lies, as many of us know, and this was a big one. Never say anything is impossible with God, for the Bible says, "Therefore, if anyone is in Christ, he is a new creation; the old has gone, the new has come!" (2 Cor. 5:17). God showed me that when we accept Christ we are new creations! In the spirit, we are clean. Many call it secondary virginity, but regardless of what name we apply, it means are we are clean and brand new. Your mind may be screaming, "That sounds good, but you cannot literally make my body virgin again." While this may be true, it disregards the fact that our bodies are temporal and the things that matter are eternal—your Spirit is eternal and God has made your Spirit brand new! Again, the promises of God are not difficult to receive; all you have to do is ask God. Ask him to make you a new creation. God will!

After you have accepted Christ as your Savior and you become a new creation, you need to break the spiritual ties you made when you had sex. Remember, in an earlier chapter I showed you that when you have sex with someone in the spirit you become one person. In order to be truly free from this spiritual tie, you need to break it. Again we are dealing in the spirit, meaning you cannot literally go back and undo the act. However, just as God has made you a new creation in the spirit, He can make you whole again by breaking off these spiritual ties you made when you had sex.

One thing I noticed through my teenage years was that after I repented for my sexual sin and I became a new creation, something still seemed lacking. It felt like part of me was clean and part of me was not. After I got married, I went through a class called Cleansing Stream, where I learned all about spiritual ties or "soul ties." I realized the reason part of me did not feel clean was because part of me was still with my other sexual partners.

The awesome thing about Jesus is that

He came to set the captives free! In Cleansing
Stream, I learned that in order to break the
spiritual ties, I needed to repent, renounce,
and break. "Repent" means to admit to our
sin and ask God's forgiveness. "Renounce"
means we talk directly to Satan and tell him
that these ties no longer have a hold on us.
Finally, we declare with our mouth that these
ties are broken. Remember, God created the
whole world with words. Your words are
powerful, and so you need to declare this
aloud. Here is what it might sound like to
break a tie.

> Lord, I repent for having sex with
> _____. I know that it was
> wrong and I am sorry for my sin with
> _____. Satan, I renounce
> all activity I have had with you in
> my sexual sin with _____.
> Satan, you no longer have a hold on

me with this sexual sin, and now in the name of Jesus Christ I break this spiritual tie with _____. I believe that I am completely whole and a new creation in Christ Jesus!

It is as simple as that. However, you have to mean it with your whole heart and believe that God has set you free. I highly recommend you do not do this alone; you should always have someone you trust to pray with you and believe with you. If you have many sex partners, write all of their names on a piece of paper and in the blanks just say, "Everyone on this list." When you are finished, rip the paper into tiny shreds and stomp on it. God instructed me to go one step beyond my sex partners and write down the names of all the people about whom I'd had sexual thoughts or with whom I'd had moments of intimacy.

The last step in the process of freedom is to be empowered by the Holy Spirit, and it is a continuous step. Once you are free from your sin, Satan will try to tempt you back into it. You can try as hard as you can to stay free on your own, but you were not meant to stand up against Satan and his tricks alone. John 16:7 says that when Jesus leaves He will send a Helper and that Helper is the Holy Spirit.

The Holy Spirit is here for all believers and will empower them to stand up against Satan and to identify Satan's tactics. To receive the Holy Spirit, all you have to do is ask. God wants all of us to walk by the Spirit, but we have to want it and ask for the Holy Spirit. The empowerment of the Holy Spirit is not a one-time event, but a continuous process. Each day you have a choice to walk by the Spirit or by the flesh. To conquer sin in your life, choose each morning to walk by the Spirit.

Some of you may think this is getting a little too deep for you. Teenagers, this stuff is real! Remember, our bodies are temporal and the spirit is eternal. Many teenagers get caught up in the moment and the here and now. Teenagers tend to have an immortality mindset—they have a long time left on this Earth, so why worry about these things now? They want to focus on what satisfies them.

Well, I am here to tell you that Satan wants to get you caught up in yourself so he can do damage to you spiritually. I know from personal experience the freedom that comes from being made whole again. No longer did part of me belong to anyone else. The amazing thing was that at the time I was going through that retreat, my husband was deployed in Turkey. So, I talked him through the process and he, too, broke the spiritual bonds we had created outside of marriage. When he came home it was like our honeymoon all over again. I had sex with my husband like it was the first time and we created the spiritual bond with each other that God talked about in Genesis and we felt no shame! From that moment on we were able to create a real intimacy with each other that extended from a physical relationship to a spiritual relationship.

Discussion Questions

1. Can you think of the last time you said or heard someone say, "What is the big deal? I was not hurting anyone?" Describe it.

2. Can you think of how that person's actions were actually hurting someone?

3. Christ has died so we could become free. Is there anyone that you created any spiritual ties with that you need to break? If so, go through the prayer on pages forty-three and forty-four and mean it in your heart.

5
Expectations

As I wrote earlier, Satan wants to get you into sexual sin and will try many ways to make it happen. One of those ways he affects people is through unrealistic expectations. In Chapter One when I told you my story, I told you how Jonathan and I both had expectations about our relationship. The problem was that we never talked about these expectations and later we found out that neither of us had wanted to do what we did. The expectations we had were completely false, but because we never

talked about them we fulfilled these false
expectations.

You may feel that was a dumb move,
something you would never do. However,
as I was studying about relationships in the
Bible, the Lord brought me to the story of
David and Bathsheba. I learned that what I
did was more common than I'd thought. Let's
look at the event to find out what I mean.

In the spring, at the time when kings go off to
war, David sent Joab out with the king's men
and the whole Israelite army. They destroyed
the Ammonites and besieged Rabbah. But
David remained in Jerusalem. One evening
David got up from his bed and walked around
on the roof of the palace. From the roof he
saw a woman bathing. The woman was very
beautiful, and David sent someone to find out
about her. The man said, "Isn't this Bathsheba,
the daughter of Eliam and the wife of Uriah

the Hittite?" Then David sent messengers
to get her. She came to him, and he slept
with her. (She had purified herself from her
uncleanness.) Then she went back home.
The woman conceived and sent word
to David, saying, "I am pregnant."

2 SAM. 11:1–5

I had read this passage many times
before, but on this occasion the Lord
showed me something. Go back through
those five verses to see when the first time
was that David and Bathsheba talked. The
verses tell us that the first words that were
communicated were, "I am pregnant." Even
then Bathsheba did not tell David in person;
she only sent word to him. Can you imagine
the expectations that were responsible for this
whole event?

Because nothing was said, everything was
based upon expectations. David called for

Bathsheba, so he already had expectations of what he wanted from her. Bathsheba was a commoner and was summoned to the king's bedroom, and I can imagine she knew exactly why she had been summoned there. Bathsheba was married and probably did not want to commit adultery with the king, but there were certain expectations when you were with the king. Surely she could not say, "King, I know you want to sleep with me, but I am married and I know committing adultery is a sin, so if you could please send me home that would be great." She probably could have been killed for denying the king. Even then, if David decided that having relations with her would be wrong, he would not have turned her away because he knew the expectations Bathsheba had of a King when summoned.

When you read further, you find that David had to go to great lengths to cover up their unplanned pregnancy, even to the point of killing someone. Letting expectations run a relationship can lead to snowballing consequences. Like David's problems kept getting bigger and bigger, consequences can keep growing in your relationship too. For example, first you lose your purity, then you end up pregnant, then your parents are disappointed in you and your relationship with them suffers. You decided to get married, but the marriage goes bad and you get a divorce; the effects could go on and on your whole life. Not to mention all the emotional and spiritual baggage you now have in your life because of all that has now happened to you.

No one plans to let expectations control their relationship. Sadly, it still occurs way too often today. I have heard countless times of youth that never talked about sex until they found out they were pregnant. If you think that expectations could never control your actions in a relationship, think again. David was considered a man after God's own heart and he still fell into the trap of expectations.

In my relationship with Jonathan, I had expected that if he wanted sex I had no choice because I was no longer a virgin and could not deny him. Jonathan expected that since I'd had sex before, I expected him to want sex. The truth was that neither of us wanted to have sex, but we each did it because we thought the other person did. We could have saved ourselves much spiritual bondage and suffering related to our actions if we had only talked about our expectations.

The only way to keep expectations from ruling your relationship is to talk about them. Talk about expectations at the beginning of the relationship, because if you wait it may be too late. Set boundaries before you begin dating. Since we know that one tactic of the enemy is to let expectations run the relationship instead of heartfelt communication, we need to be intelligent warriors to combat Satan's attacks. Communication is the key for any relationship to be healthy and in God's will. Do not let Satan get you into a life of sin. Set boundaries and communicate them clearly.

Discussion Questions

1. Think of a time when unrealistic expectations ruined a relationship in your life.

2. Think of a time when a disagreement could have been avoided if there would have been clearer communication.

3. How do you think clear communication could have changed the outcome for David and Bathsheba?

6
Making Boundaries Work in Your Relationships

Before You Start Dating

The first step toward having successful boundaries in your relationships is to start discovering your boundaries before you start dating. The only way boundaries will work in your relationships is if you actually want them. I have encountered youth that hate

when I talk about boundaries in relationships
and I've always wondered why. I thought,
"Why would someone be so opposed to
thinking about boundaries and making
a plan, if they want to stay pure before
marriage?" I found out after talking with them
that they actually did not want boundaries.
They wanted to be able to do what felt good.
They did not want hindrances in their lives.
They thought that in the heat of the moment
they could make rational decisions. They
liked the idea of staying pure, but in reality
they wanted to do what felt good in the
moment—and what if having sex felt good
in the moment? Therefore, the only way
boundaries will work for you is if your desire
is to follow God's will for your life and stay
pure.

Understanding why you want to stay
pure is a huge factor in actually staying pure.
When I was young, the only reason I wanted

to stay pure was because I was told it was right. I had no personal conviction from God. I had no clue why it was important to stay pure. Since I had no conviction in my heart about sex and purity, it was no big deal when I had sex. If you are reading this and have no conviction in your heart about staying pure, I suggest you re-read Chapter 2 and Chapter 3. Then pray and ask God to show you how important it is to stay pure.

Once you understand why you want to stay pure until marriage, you can decide what type of boundaries you want to set. There is no special code as to what purity means, and each person has their own concept of purity. I get asked all the time whether purity means doing everything except having sex. Teenagers want a clear definition of purity so they can do everything up to a certain point. The problem is that purity is a matter of the heart.

> **You have heard that it was said, "Do not commit adultery." But I tell you that anyone who looks at a woman lustfully has already committed adultery with her in his heart.**
>
> MATT. 5:27

If you do everything but have sex, I ask you where your heart is. Have you already had sex in your heart?

The best way to understand what purity means to you is to first ask God what your personal boundaries should be. Remember that when Jesus left, God gave us a Helper, the Holy Spirit. John 16 says, "[The Holy Spirit] will guide you in all truth," and James 1:5 says, "But if any of you lack wisdom, let him ask of God, who gives it to all men generously." To find out the will of God for your boundaries, all you have to do is ask God and listen to His answer.

Next, think about how much of yourself

you want to give only to your husband when
you get married, and what you would like
your husband to save for you. Most high
school relationships do not last until marriage,
and when you are in that relationship you
have to ask yourself if this how you would
have wanted your future husband or wife to
be treated by their girlfriend or boyfriend. If
the answer is no, you have discovered one
of your boundaries. For example, men, think
about your future spouse. How much of their
body do you want someone else to have
experienced? If you want your futures wives
private parts to be seen by you only, then
make sure that is one of your boundaries in
your dating relationship. The same is true for
girls; think about your future husbands and
set boundaries accordingly.

Once you have figured out your
boundaries you are ready to make a plan
to follow them. I have included a pre-dating

worksheet in Appendix A to help you write out your boundaries and make a plan for keeping them. For example, if one of your boundaries is not to see your partner naked, you would want to make a plan that does not open up those doors. For instance, you may plan to never be home alone together, or never go into each other's bedroom with the door closed. The more you think situations through, the better prepared you will be to handle those situations if they arise.

During a Dating Relationship

Once you have started a dating relationship, hopefully you have already gone through and decided upon your own desired boundaries. If you have not, it is not too late. Take some time and work through the pre-dating worksheet in Appendix A. Both partners should complete the pre-dating worksheet, even if you have been dating for a while.

When you first start a relationship, you can feel like you are in a "honeymoon period" where everything is perfect and no one wants to stir the waters. You are finally getting to know each other better and you are starting to define who you are as a couple. Your boundaries and expectations must be discussed during this time. If you feel like it is too awkward to talk about boundaries, you are not ready to date.

Avoiding uncomfortable subjects weakens your relationship. If the person you are dating does not take your boundaries seriously, drop them like a bad habit. They are a waste of your time. If they cannot respect you when you are dating, they will not respect you ever. I do not care how cute they are:

> **"Beauty is fleeting, but a [man or] woman**
> **who fears the Lord is to be praised."**
>
> Prov. 31:30

The best way to discuss boundaries with your partner is to set a date to discuss them. Make it clear that the sole purpose of the date is to discuss boundaries for your dating relationship. Making your intentions clear gives your partner time to think about his or her boundaries so they are not caught off guard by the subject. It is a good idea to give your partner a copy of the pre-dating worksheet so they can be prepared. Then, when you have your boundaries date, you can work through Appendix B. Appendix B is a worksheet for you and your partner to work through to help set boundaries and discuss expectations in your relationship.

Circumstances and situations change and it is always a good idea to review your boundaries and expectations with your partner. One way to make sure each of you keeps in tune with what is going on with the other is to keep the lines of communication open about boundaries and expectations. You may want to make it part of your anniversary celebrations to review and revise your boundaries worksheet in Appendix B.

Post-Dating Relationship

Everyone knows the saying, "You live and you learn." It is especially true in dating relationships. Now you have had time to see what goes on in dating and see how you respond to various situations. You have had time to learn what you do and do not want in your next dating relationship. Appendix C contains a worksheet for post-dating.

For these worksheets to be most effective, you need to be honest. The more honest and transparent you are in completing these worksheets, the better results you will have. This is especially true in post-dating. Everything can be a learning experience if you let it be.

Realistic Ways to Keep Your Boundaries

Boundaries are great to talk about in theory but can be hard to live out if you do not have a plan in practice. If one of your boundaries is not to see each other naked, but you are constantly home alone together, your chances of honoring that boundary is slim. This is why it is a good idea to make your boundaries known to your parents and friends. The more people that know about your boundaries the more people there are to hold you accountable.

Two practical tips when you are dating

are to never be alone together and always have something to hold you accountable. For instance, if you want private time for just the two of you, plan something where you can have a private conversation but still be publicly seen. Great places to do this are restaurants or coffee houses. Most people can have good conversations at restaurants and do not compromise boundaries. When you are at each other's houses, try to avoid the bedrooms, and if you must go in do not close the door. If you are watching movies together, do it in the living room without a blanket covering you. If you are cold, get separate blankets for each of you.

Also, watch how much time you spend together. I know it is hard to believe, but life does exist if you do not spend every waking moment with your boyfriend or girlfriend. Teenagers get easily bored and if you are constantly together you will be tempted to explore areas you would normally not have explored otherwise. It is also not healthy for you to consume your life with only one person. Make it a point to spend quality time with your other friends as well.

All relationships need a healthy balance. Try to make your relationships like scales with equal amounts of weight on each side. If you start spending too much time with one person, your scales will be unbalanced. I have often seen teens get so attached to their partner that they completely neglect their other friendships. Eventually, they end up losing their friends. All they have is their boyfriend or girlfriend and now they are scared of losing them because they are all they have. In the end, they choose to compromise their boundaries in an effort to try and keep that person around.

Telephone and Internet time also needs to be used in moderation. Just because they

are your boyfriend or girlfriend doesn't mean
they need to know every detail of your life.
Girls, men are hunters by nature and they like
to search and work for things. Leave some
things for them to find. What happens when
you completely lay your heart out on the
table and they break up with you? You are
devastated and wish you hadn't told them
so much. Not until a person has proven
him or herself trustworthy should you start
telling them intimate details about your life.
The fact that they have asked you to be their
boyfriend or girlfriend does not make them
trustworthy.

Another reason you want to limit your
telephone and Internet time with them is
because you can get easily bored after talking
for hours on end. This puts you in the same
situation as being together too much. You
may compromise physical boundaries in the
physical sense by being together too much.

Likewise, on the phone you can compromise mental boundaries. Remember when I said purity is a matter of the heart? If you are talking dirty to each other on the phone, your heart can be easily led astray.

You also want to be careful about what you allow yourself to put in your mind. If you are constantly watching movies or listening to music that promotes pre-marital sex, it will be hard to stay pure. You know the saying, "You are what you eat!" It is the same with what you put into your mind. If you put in thoughts and pictures of pure relationships, you will have pure relationships. If you put in thoughts and pictures of impurity, you will have impure relationships.

Along these same lines, you must be mindful who you hang around with. If all your friends have had sex, you will feel like the odd one out and feel pressure to have sex. Psalm 1:1 says, "Blessed is the man who does not walk in the counsel of the wicked or stand in the way of sinners or sit in the seat of mockers."

This verse gives us a picture of how a person falls. It would look something like this: You are a Christian and love the Lord. Basically, you are running with God. Then, you start listening to the counsel of the wicked and suddenly you have slowed to a walk with God. Next, you start hanging around sinners and you find yourself simply standing with God. Finally, you start doing some of the bad things your friends are doing and now you are sitting stuck going nowhere with God.

If you want to be blessed in your walk in purity, you need to stay away from the counsel of the wicked. That means you do not go to people for advice who do not have the same value of purity as you do. Surround yourself with friends that will encourage you in your walk of purity. Find older adults to confide in when you have questions and are unsure about purity. Do not seek counsel from people who do not have a strong Christian walk or you to could become stuck going nowhere with God.

Purity is a lot like the principle of reaping what you sow. If you plant tomato seeds, you harvest tomato plants. It would be crazy to plant tomato seeds and expected to grow carrots. It is the same with what you allow in your mind. If you plant seeds of impurity, you will reap fruits of impurity. When you plant seeds of purity, you will reap fruits of purity. Many youth think it is no big deal; they think that they are listening to the music but not the words. I am here to tell you it is a big deal and the words do impact you. Garbage in, garbage out!

Some of you may think some of these

suggestions are going overboard. However, in the society we live in, impurity is all around us. It is becoming more and more abnormal to desire purity. Sometimes it takes drastic measures to stand up for what's right in the culture we live in. For example, let's say you are an avid technology fan who always wants the newest gadget out there. You work really hard staying on top of the technology changes and you work hard physically to purchase all of the newest things. You do a lot of research on the products you want to purchase and you make a plan for how you will be able to purchase them. The same thing is true with purity. Purity will not just happen for you because you want it; you need to have a plan in order to stay pure.

People toss the word purity around like it is no big deal. People think anyone can stay pure if they want to. I am sorry to tell you, but it is a lie. Staying pure in this culture is hard. Staying pure may be one of the hardest things you ever do. The good news is that you can stay pure, if you do your research and make a plan.

Discussion Questions

1. Can you say wholeheartedly that you have a desire to stay pure? If not, why?

2. Have you ever had a meaningful discussion about boundaries with your parents? What were their feelings on the topic?

3. Think of three things in your life right now that negatively affect you in your walk with purity.

Appendix A
Pre-Dating
Worksheet

If you are in a relationship or are starting a
new one, you and your partner should both
complete this worksheet. When you are
finished, complete the couple's worksheet
together.

Questions:

1. What personal boundaries do you want
    to keep while you are dating? Include
    physical boundaries, communication

boundaries (phone, computer), time
boundaries, public boundaries, religious
boundaries, and any others that are
important to you.

_____

_____

_____

_____

_____

_____

_____

_____

_____

_____

2. Why are these boundaries important?

_____

_____

_____

_____

_____

_____

_____

_____

_____

_____

3. What are some practical ways you can
   implement these boundaries?
   (Example: Never be alone together.)

_____

_____

_____

_____

_____

_____

_____

_____

4. In your opinion, what is the purpose of dating and how should it affect your life?

_____

_____

_____

_____

_____

_____

_____

_____

_____

_____

Appendix B
Dating Worksheet

Questions:

1. What are your goals for this dating
   relationship?

   _____

   _____

   _____

   _____

   _____

   _____

   _____

   _____

2. What boundaries will you set in order to
    meet these goals? Include all boundaries
    discussed in your pre-dating worksheet.

    _____

    _____

    _____

    _____

    _____

    _____

    _____

    _____

    _____

    _____

3. How will you make sure these boundaries
    are honored?

    _____

    _____

    _____

    _____

_____
_____
_____
_____
_____
_____

4. What expectations do you have of each
   other?

_____
_____
_____
_____
_____
_____
_____
_____

5. Make a list of other people you know
    who you could enlist to help you adhere
    to your boundaries. (Example: parents,
    youth leaders, etc.)

    _____

    _____

    _____

    _____

    _____

    _____

    _____

    _____

    _____

    _____

These answers can be revised at anytime if
you feel like some of the boundaries are not
working or you need to add different ones.

Appendix C
Post-Dating
Worksheet

Questions:

1. What boundaries did you set for your
   relationship? Boundaries to think about:
   How much time would did spend
   together in a week? What were your
   physical intimacy boundaries (holding
   hands, touching, kissing, etc.)? How
   much time did you spend talking on the
   phone or computer to each other? How

late was too late to talk to each other?
What public displays of affection were
acceptable? Any other boundaries?

_____

_____

_____

_____

_____

_____

_____

_____

_____

_____

2. Were these boundaries discussed or
   simply implied?

_____

_____

_____

_____

_____
_____
_____
_____
_____
_____
_____

3. What boundaries would you have
    changed in your relationship and why?

_____
_____
_____
_____
_____
_____
_____
_____
_____

4. Realistically, what would have needed to change in your relationship for those changed boundaries to work?

_____

_____

_____

_____

_____

_____

_____

_____

_____

5. What type of person were you when you were in this relationship? (Examples: depressed and angry, extremely happy, or anything in between.) Why do you think you were like that?

_____

_____

_____
_____
_____
_____
_____
_____
_____
_____

6. What expressed and implied expectations
    did you have for each other in your
    relationship?

_____
_____
_____
_____
_____
_____
_____